IN THIS SERIES

Auto Racing

Baseball

Basketball

Bodybuilding

Extreme Sports

Field Hockey

Figure Skating

Football

Golf

Gymnastics

Hockey

Lacrosse

Martial Arts

Soccer

Softball

Strongman Competition

Tennis

Track and Field

Volleyball

Wrestling

THE COMPOSITE GUIDE

to FIELD HOCKEY

BRUCE ADELSON

CHELSEA HOUSE PUBLISHERS

Philadelphia

Produced by Choptank Syndicate, Inc. and Chestnut Productions

Senior Editor: Norman L. Macht
Editor and Picture Researcher: Mary E. Hull
Design and Production: Lisa Hochstein
Cover Illustrator: Cliff Spohn

Project Editor: Jim McAvoy
Art Direction: Sara Davis
Cover Design: Keith Trego

First Printing

1 3 5 7 9 8 6 4 2

Library of Congress Cataloging-in-Publication Data

Adelson, Bruce.
    The composite guide to field hockey / by Bruce Adelson.
        p. cm.—(The composite guide)
    Includes bibliographical references and index.
    ISBN 0-7910-5863-8
    1. Field hockey—Juvenile literature. I. Title: Field hockey. II. Title. III. Series.
GV1017.H7 A34 2000
646.7'5—dc21

                               99-086455

CONTENTS

1 AN EXCITING GAME

Field Hockey has been around for thousands of years. Played on an open, outdoor field with sticks and round balls, it is a fast-paced game, with players running up and down the field trying to score goals. Field hockey games are usually low scoring contests, with plenty of good defense and goalkeeping. Scores of 1–0, 2–0, or 2–1 are typical.

The sport is played by men and women around the world—in North America, South America, Europe, Asia, and the Australian continent. One of the best, most exciting games in recent field hockey history took place in 1999 at the Pan American Games in Winnipeg, a city in the Canadian province of Manitoba. Canada and Argentina played each other for the gold medal.

In recent years, Canada and Argentina have become powerful field hockey competitors. Their national teams have played against each other several times in international competition. Argentina defeated Canada for the Pan American gold medal in 1991 and 1995. Argentina also beat Canada, 1–0, in 1996, a victory which sent Argentina to the 1996 Olympics. Canada beat Argentina in 1998 while both countries were trying to qualify for the field hockey World Cup.

In 1999 Canada and Argentina were considered the favorites to compete for the Pan American gold medal. During the tournament, they were

Andrew Griffiths (#8) of Canada moves the ball as Carlos Retegui of Argentina tries to defend during the men's field hockey gold medal match at the August 4, 1999, Pan Am Games in Winnipeg, Canada.

the best teams, each finishing with five wins, zero losses, and one tie before facing each other in the final round.

A lot was at stake in the 1999 championship game. Since 1979, Canada and Argentina had played six international tournament championship round games against each other. Each team had won three times. In 1999 at the Pan American Games, both teams had a chance to break this 3–3 tie and have more wins than its rival. The winner of the Pan American gold medal would also be allowed to compete at the 2000 Olympic Games in Sydney, Australia.

The Canadian men's field hockey team had not played in the Olympics since 1988, so they were determined not to let this chance at Olympic competition slip away.

When the game started, the small Winnipeg field hockey stadium was packed with people. More than 2,000 screaming fans jammed into a stadium that normally could seat about 1,500 people. They were cheering for their countrymen, waving Canadian flags and getting ready for an exciting game. With Argentina as the opponent, everyone thought the game would be close and hard fought.

Before the game started, 23-year-old Canadian goalie Mike Mahood attached a small object to his goal for good luck. It was a dream catcher, made by Canadian Indians. Mahood, a University of British Columbia student who put his education on hold to pursue a shot at the Olympics, put the dream catcher there as a symbol, hoping it would catch the dreams of Canada's team to win the game and go on to the 2000 Olympics.

The game began and both teams tried to score the first goal. In field hockey, because games are low scoring, one goal is often all that is scored by both teams. After about 30 scoreless minutes, there was a scramble for the ball in front of Argentina's goalkeeper, Marino Chao. The ball rebounded from Chao and shot back into the field. Canada's Ken Pereira stopped the ball with his stick and then

Still wearing his leg pads, goalie Mike Mahood of the Canadian men's field hockey team carries the Canadian flag as he and his teammates celebrate their victory over Argentina at the Pan Am Games in Winnipeg.

shot it back toward Chao. The ball rocketed through players standing in front of Chao and shot into the goal. Canada scored and led Argentina, 1–0. The fans cheered wildly, excited that their national team had scored the game's first goal. They cheered even louder when the first half ended with Canada holding a 1–0 lead. Twenty-six-year-old Pereira had scored perhaps the most important goal in his field hockey career. As he later told reporters, the ball "hit a couple of sticks. Andrew Griffiths took a swipe at it first, it hit the goalie and came back to my stick. I flicked it and saw it go in. That was the best feeling I've had in my entire life. I hadn't scored all tournament and I kept telling the guys I was saving it for the final, and I did it."

Maybe Pereira was helped by his usual pregame meal: before every game, he ate the same thing, pasta and a glazed doughnut.

Although the fans and Canadian players were very excited about the 1–0 score, there was still plenty of the game left to play. After a halftime break, both teams had to play a 35-minute second half.

Argentina charged onto the field to start the second half. They rushed up and down the field and pushed hard to score a goal. With about five minutes left in the game, one hard shot got past Canadian goalie Mike Mahood, but it did not go into the goal. The ball hit one of the goal posts, which Mahood had nick-named "Frank," and ricocheted away from the goal. Canada was still winning, 1–0. Mahood, who is a superstitious player, was very grate-ful that his friend "Frank" helped keep Argentina from scoring.

But the Argentine team did not stop. As the game's minutes ticked away, their players kept coming on strong, trying hard to tie the game. Mahood played one of the best games of his career. He stopped every ball the Argentinians shot at him. By the end of the game, he had 13 saves. With only seconds left to play, the Canadians knew they were going to win. As the game ended, the small stadium became a place of wild celebration and fans waved the red and white Canadian maple leaf flag to celebrate their team's exciting 1–0 victory.

The Canadian players were jubilant. They jumped up and down, hugging each other. Before celebrating with his teammates, Mike Mahood took off his goalie mask and ran toward the stands with his arms raised over his head. Screaming happily, he did not stop when he reached the fence. Still wearing his long leg pads, he jumped over the fence, landing in the first row of seats. He quickly stood up and looked for his family. "I had to go see Mom," he told a reporter from the Canadian Press later on, "She was the biggest supporter of all." Canada's gold medal-winning field hockey goalie finally found his mother. Still wearing his uniform and pads, he gave her and the rest of his family big hugs.

This was a particularly special moment for Mahood. He had been criticized in 1998 for getting into a fight with a player from the Malaysian team after a game in Kuala Lumpur, the capital of Malaysia. Since that incident, Mahood had tried to convince people he was a dedicated, hardworking player, and that he could control his emotions. Finally, with his remarkable shutout of the Argentine team,

Mahood was vindicated. With the Canadian team's victory over Argentina in this exciting and difficult game, Canada's dream of participating in the 2000 Olympic Games would now come true.

After celebrating with his family, Mahood joined his teammates on the field. They ran around the stadium cheering, shaking a Canadian flag, and waving to the fans while the song "We Are the Champions" was played over the loudspeakers. The players began dancing across the field as the celebration continued. Mahood told a reporter from the *Toronto Sun*, "I'm absolutely thrilled. We put so much work in for this. This means so much to everybody."

In contrast to other sports like football or ice hockey, field hockey players do not earn much money playing the game. They play because they love the sport. They play on national teams to honor their countries.

Canadian field hockey team captain Peter Milkovich told reporters in 1999, "We've sacrificed careers, girlfriends, [and] jobs. We [don't play hockey] for money. There's no money in field hockey. We do it because we love the game and wanted to be there for Canada. The next thing is to build this team into an Olympic contender."

As Canadian coach Shiaz Virjee told the *Toronto Sun*, "These guys played their hearts out. . . . These guys have not only dedicated themselves but they've been forking out their own money to keep this thing going for years. We took money out of our own pockets just to buy shirts for the volunteers around the team and had to buy our own uniforms."

This game showcased the best field hockey has to offer—a great defense and excellent goal-keeping in a close, tense, low scoring contest between two field hockey powerhouses. It will be remembered as one of the best in the sport's 4,000 year history.

THE HISTORY OF FIELD HOCKEY

Field hockey is one of the oldest games that people still play. In fact, this sport may be thousands of years older than football, baseball, soccer, or ice hockey.

It is hard to say exactly when field hockey was first invented. But we do know that this game is older than the ancient Olympic Games, which began in Athens, Greece, in 776 B.C. Archaeologists have found drawings of men playing a type of field hockey in the tomb of Beni-Hasen, an ancient Egyptian who died about 4,000 years ago.

Over the centuries, many peoples have played this historic game. Experts have found proof that the ancient Greeks, Romans, Persians, Arabs, Europeans, Ethiopians, and Native Americans all played forms of field hockey.

Arabic people used curved sticks and balls made from palm fibers and esparto grass. Hurling, a sport like field hockey, was played in Ireland around 1000 B.C. Aztec Indians had been playing field hockey in the New World for centuries before Christopher Columbus arrived there in 1492.

Native peoples in North and South America played field hockey with sticks made from animal bones. Their version of field hockey was called shinny. In this game, players could not touch the ball with their hands. Players hit the ball with a curved stick, much like today's field

At the beginning of the 20th century, women field hockey players wore long skirts or baggy knickers and long-sleeved shirts or sweaters during games. Dressed in the sports attire of their time, these women face off at a 1919 game.

Male members of "the club of true highlanders" play an early version of field hockey in this 1845 illustration.

hockey stick, and tried to shoot it into the other team's goal. The carved shinny sticks were usually between two and four feet long. They were painted with bright colors and symbols that told a story about each stick's owner.

Shinny balls were made from deer or buckskin. They were often hollow and came in different sizes, ranging from as large as a baseball to as small as a golf ball. Like the shinny sticks, each ball was also painted with decorations and symbols of special importance.

Native Americans played shinny on a field shaped like a rectangle. Fields were of many different sizes. They could be as short as 200 yards, which is double the length of today's football fields, or as long as a mile.

The smallest teams usually had about 10 players, close to the 11 players a standard field hockey team has today. Sometimes, each shinny team had as many as 100 players, making the field a very crowded place. This

was why some fields were up to a mile long: the teams needed plenty of room with 100 players on each side.

From 500 to 1500 A.D., medieval Europeans played field hockey in many different countries, including England, France, and Scotland. A stick-and-ball game was played in England as early as 1175. Thirteenth-century stained glass windows at Canterbury and Gloucester Cathedrals in England depict boys hitting balls with curved sticks. The games were called different names—bandy in Wales, hurley or hurling in Ireland, and shinty in Scotland.

Field hockey did not get its name until the 1700s. The word "hockey" is believed to come

Jacques Grasset de Saint-Sauveur included this image of Native Americans playing lacrosse in his Tableaux Cosmographiques, *published in 1787. The Native American game of lacrosse is very similar to field hockey.*

from the French word "hoquet," which means a shepherd's crook or staff, used for herding sheep or other animals. When the French played field hockey, they called it hoquet.

The modern game of field hockey was invented in England in the 1800s. Games were played at public schools on open fields.

At first, modern field hockey was played only by men. They believed the sport was too rough for women. In the 1800s, many men also believed that women were not physically strong enough to play most sports. At that time, women were restricted to playing croquet and lawn tennis. Men thought women could handle these games because they did not involve any physical contact or a lot of running and jumping.

The first field hockey club—Blackheath—was formed in England in 1849. The Blackheath team used a square of solid black rubber as the ball. Another team, called Teddington, is credited with turning field hockey into a modern game. Based in London, Teddington's players introduced several new rules to the sport, such as preventing players from lifting their sticks above the shoulder or using their hands to advance the ball down the field. Unlike Blackheath, they used a round ball. In 1875 the Men's Hockey Association of London published several rules for the sport, establishing the size of the field and reducing the number of players on each team.

The success of Blackheath, Teddington, and other London teams led to the formation in London of the first field hockey league, the Hockey Association, in 1886. The British Army introduced modern field hockey to men in different countries over the next several years, leading to the first international field hockey tournament in 1895.

By 1887 women began making their mark in the sport. That year, the first women's field hockey team was started in the town of East Mosley, England. Women enjoyed this new, fast-moving sport. The All England Women's Hockey Association was formed in 1889. Five years later, the Irish Ladies Hockey Union began to play.

Even though women played field hockey just like men, there were certain rules they alone had to follow. Women were not permitted to wear shorts, short skirts, or short-sleeved uniform tops. Instead, they wore long skirts and long-sleeved shirts or sweaters. Many people in the late 19th and early 20th centuries felt it was improper for women to reveal too much of themselves. Unlike female athletes today, who wear comfortable uniforms that allow them to move their arms and legs freely, the early women field hockey players had to wear heavy, long clothing, which made running difficult.

Constance Applebee, a teacher at the British College of Physical Education, brought field hockey to the United States in 1901. Born in England, Constance Applebee came to the United States to take a class at Harvard University in Boston, Massachusetts. During a class discussion about women's exercises, the teacher talked about games the U.S. women played, such as musical chairs and an old-fashioned game called "drop the handkerchief." After hearing about the sports American women played, Applebee became concerned that

Constance Applebee, right, receives flowers from Philadelphia Field Hockey Association President Jen Shillingford in 1967. Known as the mother of modern field hockey, Applebee brought the sport to women's collegiate athletics in the U.S. and cofounded the United States Field Hockey Association.

women in this country were not getting proper exercise. She decided to change that. When asked what games women played in England, she talked about field hockey. Constance Applebee then decided to show her classmates how to play the game.

One day, during a class break, she borrowed some hockey sticks and indoor baseballs. She then took a piece of chalk and marked off a hockey field outside Harvard's gymnasium. There, she put on the first modern field hockey demonstration in the United States, showing women in her class how to play what was for them a brand new sport. Her "students" were very excited about the chance to play a competitive, fast-moving athletic game for the first time in their lives.

Constance Applebee showed women at other American colleges and universities how to play field hockey. In 1901 she went to Vassar College in New York, where she found 24 hockey sticks left behind by an Englishman who had tried unsuccessfully to interest American men in the game. But Constance Applebee had more success than her countryman. American women quickly became enthusiastic players. She gave field hockey clinics at several other women's colleges, including Smith, Wellesley, Mount Holyoke, and Radcliffe. Thanks to Constance Applebee, several colleges and clubs sponsored women's field hockey teams in the United States by the early 1920s. A U.S. women's touring field hockey team played in its first international competition in 1920.

In 1904, Applebee became the director of outdoor sports at Bryn Mawr College in Pennsylvania. Two years later, she became that school's physical education director. In 1922, while working at Bryn Mawr, she and 12 other women founded the United States Field Hockey Association (USFHA) in Philadelphia. Today, this association governs women's field hockey and helps promote and support the sport around the country.

Constance Applebee also started a field hockey camp while she worked at Bryn Mawr. In 1923, over 300 women from England came to this camp to learn about the game.

In her 40-year coaching career at Ursinus College, Eleanor Snell coached four women's sports—field hockey, softball, basketball, and tennis—and never had a losing season.

During World War II, Applebee raised money in the United States to be used for ambulances to transport wounded soldiers from the battlefield to a hospital. Four of the ambulances sent to England from the United States had a message on the side: "Donated by the Women Hockey Players of the U.S.A."

Applebee, also known affectionately as "the Apple" to her thousands of students, helped teach field hockey and other sports to women at Bryn Mawr for almost 70 years, until 1971, when she was 97 years old. In 1980, the Association for Intercollegiate Athletics for Women presented her with its Award for Merit in recognition of her contribution to women's athletics in the United States. In 1981, Constance Applebee, regarded as the mother of modern field hockey, died in England at the age of 107.

One of the women who learned about field hockey from Constance Applebee was Eleanor Snell, who became one of the greatest coaches in American field hockey history. While coaching at Ursinus College in Pennsylvania for 38 years, she produced teams that won 198 games and lost only 61. Her teams never had a losing record. During the 1960s, the Ursinus Bears lost only six games, going undefeated from 1960 through 1964. After a loss in 1965, "Snell's Belles" began another streak of 36 games without a loss before bowing to West Chester University, 7–1. The following year they again went undefeated, outscoring their opponents 35–1 in nine games.

During Snell's time at Ursinus, the school had the best women's teams in the country. They went undefeated 12 times and had 14 seasons in which they lost only one game each year.

But Eleanor Snell did more than coach field hockey at Ursinus. She also coached the college's women's softball, basketball, and tennis teams. Eleanor Snell's record as a coach for all these teams is an incredible 674 wins, 194 losses and 42 ties. To commemorate the school's legendary coach, Ursinus College competes annually in field hockey against another college team for the Snell Cup, named in honor of Eleanor Snell.

Ursinus was a great field hockey power in the 1960s and most of the 1970s. But the college was defeated at the 1976 and '77 Women's Field Hockey Championships by West Chester University of Pennsylvania. Ursinus returned to national field hockey prominence in 1983. That year, led by 5' 1" Kelee Whiteley, the team's top scorer, Ursinus captured the East Coast Athletic Conference Division I Field Hockey Championship. To get to the championship, Ursinus defeated Boston College in a semifinal match. Then, in an exciting final game, Ursinus beat Northeastern University, 4–3, in a game that went into three overtime periods. In 1984 Ursinus finished second to Boston College for the championship. When the 1984 U.S. women's field hockey team won the Olympic bronze medal, five of the players were alumnae of Ursinus College.

West Chester University is Ursinus College's archrival. That is not surprising because they are both located near Philadelphia, which is one of the country's field hockey capitals. The Field Hockey Hall of Fame is located on the Ursinus College campus. Regionally, the sport is played by girls and women from elementary school through college, and there are many amateur field hockey clubs in the area.

West Chester and Ursinus have played against each other each year since 1939, and they have one of the longest-running field hockey rivalries in American college sports. One memorable contest occurred on November 6, 1992. On a cold day in front of only 24 fans, Ursinus and West Chester played a thrilling, close game. After 70 minutes, the score was tied, 2–2. To break the tie, the teams then played a 15-minute sudden death overtime. The first team to score would win the game.

The 1915 Vassar College women's field hockey team pose in their uniforms. Vassar was one of the first women's colleges in the United States to introduce field hockey.

The first overtime was scoreless. As the weather grew colder, the teams began playing a second overtime period. Finally, after a little more than six minutes of the second overtime period, Trisha Davies, a senior player for West Chester, scored the game-winning goal.

Unlike American women, American men did not like field hockey very much at first. But men from other countries felt differently. In 1924 the Federation Internationale de Hockey sur Gazon was formed to supervise men's field hockey around the world. The first game between two men's teams in the United States took place in 1928 when the Westchester, New York, Field Hockey Club played the Germantown, Pennsylvania, Cricket Club.

In 1928 the Field Hockey Association of America (FHAA) was formed to regulate men's field hockey and promote the sport in the United States. In 1930 the FHAA joined the Federation Internationale de Hockey. Today more than 100 nations belong to this federation.

Men's field hockey became an Olympic sport in 1908. It took more than 70 years for women's teams to be allowed to compete. At the 1980 Olympic Games in Moscow, which were boycotted by the United States, the first women's Olympic field hockey teams played. At the 2000 Olympics in Sydney, Australia, there were 12 men's teams and 10 women's teams. At the 2004 Olympic Games in Athens, there will be 12 field hockey teams for both men and women.

More than 11,000 players and coaches now belong to the United States Field Hockey Association. About 3,000 American high

Though men's field hockey became an Olympic sport in 1908, it took longer to catch on in the U.S. than women's field hockey did. This photo shows the American men's team playing Great Britain in 1937.

schools and colleges have field hockey teams, with more than 200 programs at universities and colleges belonging to the National Collegiate Athletic Association. A large number of schools belonging to the smaller National Association of Intercollegiate Athletics also play field hockey.

Millions of people participate in field hockey in more than 90 countries. Currently, countries like the Netherlands, Germany, South Korea, New Zealand, Spain, Australia, England, Pakistan, and India have some of the strongest field hockey teams in international competition. There are many international tournaments, including the Pan American Games, Asian Games, African Games, and the

Inter-Continental Cup. As the sport continues to grow in popularity, new competitions are organized. Men and women enjoy field hockey all over the world. But in the United States, the sport is played primarily by women.

3 PLAYING THE GAME

The object of field hockey is easy to understand. Players use wooden sticks to hit a small ball into a net and score a goal. Field hockey games are usually played outside on grass or artificial turf fields. The field is a rectangle, 60 yards wide and 100 yards long, the same length as a football field. One goal cage stands at each end of the field. Each cage is seven feet high and four feet wide. In front of the cage, there is a semicircle, also called the striking or shooting circle, which extends 16 yards onto the field. Besides the striking circle, there is a centerline drawn across the middle of the field where each game starts and where play begins again after each goal. There are also two 25-yard lines drawn in front of each striking circle.

Each team has 10 players and one goalkeeper. These 10 players usually include five forwards or attackers, who have the job of trying to score goals, three halfbacks, and two fullbacks, whose job is to play defense and prevent the other team from scoring. The number of players at these positions often changes during games, depending on what their team needs them to do. For uniforms and equipment, players usually wear shirts, shorts, or skirts (for women) plus mouth and shin guards. Field hockey goalkeepers, like ice hockey goalies, wear thick pads on their legs as well as protective face masks and thick gloves.

Australia's defense, led by Kate Starr, left, and goalkeeper Karon Marsdon (9), waits inside the goal cage for an attack during their match with the Netherlands at the 1996 Olympics in Atlanta, Georgia. In order to score a goal in field hockey, the entire ball must pass over the goal line.

Each player carries a short hardwood stick that is 36 inches long. The sticks are very light, weighing no more than 1 1/2 pounds for women and almost two pounds for men. The bottom of the stick, the part players use to hit the ball, is curved on one side and flat on the other. The balls look like baseballs. Field hockey balls can have hollow centers or they can be made of twine and cork or solid plastic. They are often covered by white leather or plastic.

Each game is divided into two 35-minute halves. There is a halftime break of 10 minutes. Two referees keep track of time, call penalties, and supervise the game. Once the game begins, there are no substitutions if a player is disqualified by a penalty—a team cannot send in a replacement for the original player. But players who are injured can be replaced. Other substitutions are limited to two at a time. The player being replaced must run completely off the field near the centerline before the substitute can come into the game. There are no time-outs. Play continues until a goal is scored or one of the referees calls time because of injury or a penalty.

A coin toss determines which team gets the ball first. The winner starts the game by hitting the ball in any direction from the centerline. The ball cannot be hit into the air but must be hit or pushed along the ground. Each team must stand on its side of the centerline with the defending team at least five yards from the ball before play can start.

During the game, players move the ball up and down the field by hitting it with their sticks. Players cannot hit the ball with their hands, legs, or other parts of their bodies.

Only the goalkeepers can use their hands or legs to block the balls or kick them away from the goal cages. Outside the striking circle, the goalkeeper is treated like any other player and can only use the stick to hit the ball.

To score a goal, the entire ball must pass over the goal line. This is different from ice hockey, where only part of the puck needs to cross the goal line. In field hockey, the ball must also have been hit by, or glance off, the stick of an attacking player inside the striking circle. Balls that are touched by defenders after being hit by an attacker and crossing the goal line are counted as goals. Any ball hit from outside the striking circle that goes into the goal cage does not count as a score.

Most goals are scored on either penalty strokes or short corners. A short corner is when an attacking player gets a free shot from at least 10 yards from the goal. All other

Canada's Jenny Zinkan-McGrade (6) and Argentina's Paula Masotta, right, lean for the ball during the final moments of their match at the 1999 Pan Am Games in Winnipeg, Canada. Argentina won, 3–1.

attackers must be outside the striking circle before the attacker hits the ball. These attackers can take any positions they want to try to fool the defenders about how the ball will be hit. Attackers usually have a plan for scoring a goal and set up their play once the referee gives the signal to begin the short corner.

The defending team can put up to four players inside the goal cage with the goalkeeper to keep the attacker from scoring. The goal cage

A German player prepares for a short corner during a game against Great Britain. When a player gets a foul in field hockey, the referee awards the opposing team with a short corner, allowing them a free shot at the other team's goal.

can look pretty crowded with all the defenders standing inside it. These defenders cannot move before the attacker shoots the ball. All other players on the defending team must stand behind the centerline.

Once the attacker hits the ball, the others can cross the striking circle and rush toward the goal cage, hoping to score. The defenders run out of the goal cage and try to steal the ball and stop the play before a goal can be scored.

Like ice hockey, field hockey has penalty shots, also called penalty strokes. Penalty strokes are called if a defender breaks a rule. The attacking player who has the penalty shot stands seven feet in front of the goal cage. The goalkeeper stands at the front of the goal, with both feet on the goal line. All other players must stand behind the 25-yard line. The attacking player cannot move the ball before shooting. The ball can be touched only once, when the shot is taken. When shooting, the player can take one forward step, but the rear foot cannot pass the front one until the shot is taken. The goalkeeper cannot move either foot until the ball is hit. If the goalkeeper commits a foul to prevent a goal from being scored during the penalty shot, the referee can award the other team a goal.

After a goal is scored, the ball is brought to the centerline, where the team that was scored against puts the ball back into play in the same way that the game began. The game can also be restarted with a bully. A bully occurs when a game is stopped for any reason other than a goal or a foul by one player, such as when the ball has to be replaced, when both teams commit fouls, or when the ball gets stuck in a player or referee's uniform. For a bully, a player stands across from his opponent at the centerline. The ball is placed between them. Before being allowed to hit the ball, each player must hit the ground with the stick and then the opponent's stick alternately three times. All other players must stand at least five yards away from the ball during the bully.

Several different fouls or penalties can be called during field hockey games. Here are the ones than happen most often:

OFF-SIDE: this is similar to ice hockey. A player is penalized for running ahead of a teammate with the ball in the defending team's half of the field, receiving the ball when fewer than three defenders are between the attacker and the goal line.

ADVANCING THE BALL: as in soccer, players cannot use their hands to advance the ball. If a ball is advanced by a player using any part of the body, a foul is called. It is not a foul if the ball hits a player's hand and then drops immediately without the player holding or advancing it.

DANGEROUS USE OF THE STICK: when a player raises the stick above the shoulder while playing the ball and hits the ball in a way which could result in a possible injury.

HOOKING: using a stick to hook or grab an opponent's stick.

OBSTRUCTION: a player is not allowed to obstruct or block an opponent by putting the stick or any part of the body between the opponent and the ball. A player may not run between the opponent and the ball. Players are not allowed to use their bodies to shield or protect the ball from an opponent. All players have the same chance to get the ball as it is passed, dribbled, or shot down the field.

If any of these fouls are called, the referee sets up a "free hit." On a free hit, the player who was fouled gets a free shot at the ball from the spot where the foul occurred, without interference from an opponent. The ball must travel at least one yard and cannot be retouched by the attacker until another player hits the ball.

Field hockey is a game of speed, strength, and skill. Players must be able to attack or defend, depending upon what their coach needs them to do in each game. Players must also follow the rules to have the best chance of helping their team win the game.

FIELD HOCKEY IN THE UNITED STATES

4

The sport of field hockey has grown in popularity since Constance Applebee introduced it to this country in 1901. Most women living in the United States today have probably played field hockey at one time in their lives—during gym class in high school or on a high school or university team. Although field hockey is no longer the only sport available to American women, it remains a popular game.

Field hockey has never really caught on with American men. This lack of popularity is one reason American men have not done well in international field hockey competitions. Since capturing the 1932 Olympic bronze medal, no U.S. men's field hockey team has won another Olympic medal. In fact, U.S. men's field hockey teams have never won a field hockey match in Olympic history. When the U.S. men won a bronze medal in 1932, there were only three teams competing, so each team was guaranteed to win either a gold, silver, or bronze. In that Olympics, the U.S. team lost the two games it played. India won the gold, Japan the silver, and the U.S. won the bronze by default.

In Olympic history, the U.S. men's teams have lost 26 games, won zero, and tied four. At the 1996 Olympics in Atlanta, the men's team lost all seven games they played. The team was outscored 26–4 and was shut out three times.

This 1936 Olympic poster shows a men's field hockey game in Berlin, Germany. Though the U.S. men's field hockey team won a bronze medal at the 1932 Olympics, no U.S. men's team has won a medal since.

The U.S. women's field hockey team plays England in a 1954 match. In the United States, where field hockey was one of the first team sports made available to women, the game has always been more popular among women than men.

U.S. women's teams have enjoyed more success than their male counterparts. In the 1996 Olympics, the women's team won fifth place by beating Spain, 2–0. But in 1984, the U.S. women's Olympic field hockey team enjoyed plenty of excitement. That year, the team became the only U.S. team to win a field hockey medal since World War II and the first U.S. team to win any individual field hockey games in Olympic history.

Nineteen eighty-four was the first year that almost all of the world's best field hockey teams competed against each other in the Olympics. Although Olympic women's field hockey began in 1980, most of the world's best teams did not participate. That year, the Olympics were held in Moscow, in what was then called the Soviet Union. Before the Olympics were scheduled to open, the Soviet

Union invaded Afghanistan, one of its neighboring countries. To express their displeasure with what the Soviet Union had done, many countries, led by the United States, boycotted, or didn't participate in, the Games.

Most of the best field hockey powers came back to the 1984 Games. The top women's teams in the world, such as the Netherlands, Australia, West Germany, Canada, and New Zealand, traveled to the United States to participate in Los Angeles, California.

On August 1, 1984, the U.S. women's team won its first game, beating Canada, 4–1. The U.S. team was led by its captain, Beth Anders, who scored three goals.

Anders, then 31 years old, was an alumna of Ursinus College and had been waiting a long time to play field hockey in the Olympics. Considered to be one of the best players in the United States, some of her shots had been clocked as fast as 75 mph. Anders also played on every U.S. World Cup team from 1971 to 1983 and was the team's leading scorer. In 1980 Anders's talents were recognized when she was named "All World Midfielder." During the 1983 World Cup Tournament, she scored six goals in seven games to help the United States finish sixth. Beth Anders was the field hockey coach at Old Dominion University in Virginia when she tried out for the Olympic team. In 1982 Old Dominion had won the National Field Hockey Championship. From 1980 to 1983, the school's team was ranked as one of the five best in the country. So when Beth Anders was the top scorer in the American team's first Olympic win, no one was really surprised.

Led by Anders's eight goals in five games—an Olympic record—the U.S. won the bronze, defeating Australia, 10–5, in their finale. The team's 5' 2" goalkeeper, Gwen Cheeseman, had played on three World Cup teams—in 1975, 1980, and 1983. In 1984 she gave up only one goal in four matches during the Four Nations International Tournament. The coach of the U.S. team that year was Vonnie Gros, another Ursinus College alumna. Before the 1984 Olympics, Gros had also coached the 1979 and 1983 World Cup squads. Gros is a member of the Field Hockey Hall of Fame.

After the Olympics, Beth Anders was again recognized for her field hockey skill. On January 21, 1985, she was honored as the Top Amateur Athlete by the Philadelphia Sports Writers Association. Since its founding in 1904, the association had never given this award to a woman. Beth Anders was inducted into the Field Hockey Hall of Fame in 1989.

But this is not the end of Beth Anders's story. She continued coaching and winning at Old Dominion University. Her teams kept capturing championships in 1988, 1990, 1991, and 1992. In her career at Old Dominion, Anders has won seven National Collegiate Athletic Association Championships. Beth Anders has won more games than any other field hockey coach who is coaching today at an American college or university. From 1990 to 1993, she was also the coach of the U.S. national field hockey team.

Although Beth Anders was a great field hockey player, another member of the Field Hockey Hall of Fame is considered by many to be the greatest player in U.S. history. Anne

Townsend was born in Philadelphia in 1900. She graduated from the University of Pennsylvania, where she was captain of the women's field hockey and basketball teams.

Townsend was selected as a member of the first 15 all-American field hockey teams, from 1924 to 1938. To be selected for the all-American field hockey team, a player must be one of the country's top field hockey players. Nicknamed "Towser," Anne was the all-American team captain all of those years except 1933. A very versatile player, she was selected as an all-American at four different positions—center halfback, left inside forward, right halfback, and right fullback. Townsend

Katie Kauffmann of the U.S., left, chases the ball with Germany's Philippa Suxdorf during their game at the 1996 summer Olympics. The U.S. women's team placed fifth in 1996.

Anne Townsend was captain of the women's all-American field hockey team for 14 years and also served as president of the United States Field Hockey Association from 1928 to 1932.

was president of the U.S. Field Hockey Association from 1928 to 1932. In 1947 she was named to the all-American team again, when she was 47 years old and playing for amateur club teams.

But Townsend was more than just a great field hockey player. She was also named to the Women's all-American Lacrosse Team in 1933, '34, '36, and '38. In 1957 she and a teammate won the National Squash Doubles Championship. At the time, Townsend was 57 years old.

After her playing career ended, Townsend coached high school field hockey teams and umpired games. One of the sport's greatest figures, Anne Townsend died in 1984. Four years after she died, Townsend was honored again when she was inducted into the Field Hockey Hall of Fame.

FIELD HOCKEY AROUND THE WORLD

5

In ancient times, field hockey-like games such as shinny, hurling, bandy, and shinty were developed and played by people all over the world. Today, modern field hockey continues to be enjoyed by people from many different cultural backgrounds. The game is played by both men and women in the Americas, Europe, Asia, Africa, and Australia. One hundred nineteen member associations from every corner of the globe belong to the International Hockey Federation, the official international governing body of field hockey. Many of the greatest games in field hockey history have been played in international competition.

As mentioned earlier, men's field hockey was first played in the modern Olympic Games in 1908. That year, the Olympics were held in London, England. English fans had a lot to cheer about, because the English team won the first ever men's field hockey gold medal, beating Ireland, 8–1.

Although England was one of the leading centers of field hockey in the late 19th century and the early 20th century, this dominance ended in the 1920s. By 1928, India, then an English colony, had become the world's greatest field hockey center.

Field hockey in India goes back more than 100 years. Today field hockey is India's national

India's Dhanaraj Pillay (right), beats Canada's Ian Bird to the ball during the Sultan Azlan Shah hockey tournament in Kuala Lumpur on February 19, 2000. By 2000, field hockey was played by men and women in over 100 countries.

sport, as ice hockey is in Canada and baseball and football are in the United States.

India's first field hockey clubs began playing in 1885 in the city of Calcutta. In 1926 India played in its first international competitions when Indian teams played against New Zealand. Two years later, at the 1928 Olympics in Amsterdam, Holland, India established itself as a world field hockey power, winning its first gold medal with five shutout victories. India's field hockey team was led by Dhyan Chand, a 22-year-old captain in the army. In his career, Chand eventually won three Olympic field hockey gold medals. After he stopped playing, he became the coach of India's national team.

Not everyone in India was aware of that country's emerging field hockey prowess. According to IndianHockey.com, the Internet home of Indian field hockey, Indian leader Mahatma Gandhi had never heard of field hockey. When asked to help raise funds to send the 1932 Olympic team to Los Angeles, Gandhi is reported to have asked "What's hockey?"

India's men's teams won the gold at the next six consecutive Olympic Games: 1932, '36, '48, '52, '56, and '60. (No Olympics were held in 1940 or 1944 because of World War II, which ended in 1945).

During India's gold medal streak, it had a record of 30 wins and no losses in Olympic competition, scoring 197 goals and giving up only eight. During India's winning streak, no opponent scored more than one goal in any game. This lasted until the 1972 Olympics, when New Zealand defeated India, 2–1, in a semifinal match.

In 1932 India set an all-time Olympic record for the most goals scored in a field hockey game when it defeated the United States, 24–1. In that game, Dhyan Chand scored eight goals, but he was not the leading scorer. His teammate, Roap Singh, scored 10 goals to help lead India to its second straight gold medal. During that Olympics, India also beat Japan, 11–1. Since field hockey games are usually low scoring contests, these scores are truly amazing.

India's field hockey team proved itself again in 1936, defeating the German team at the Berlin Olympics, 8–1. Trailing Germany, 1–0,

The Indian men's field hockey team competes at the 1936 Olympics in Berlin, Germany, where they took home the gold medal.

in the first half, India scored eight straight goals, led by Chand, who scored six goals while playing barefoot.

India became an independent country in 1948. That year, England played its former colony in field hockey for the first time. Not wanting to be embarrassed by losing to its colony, England had always avoided playing the world champion Indian team. India shut out England, 4–0, in the 1948 Olympics and won another gold medal.

India's dominance of field hockey faltered in 1960, when it faced Pakistan for the gold medal. Although India had a great team, Pakistan was not bullied. Pakistan began the game playing hard, surprising the Indians with how strongly they were competing. After 12 minutes of the game had gone by, Pakistan's

During a ceremony at the 1996 summer Olympics in Atlanta, members of the Australian women's field hockey team celebrate their gold medal victory over South Korea.

Nasir Ahmad scored the game's only goal. Pakistan won the gold medal, and India lost for the first time in more than 30 years.

Pakistan's 1960 victory over India was the beginning of a great field hockey rivalry between these two countries. India beat Pakistan, 1–0, for the gold medal in 1964, when player Mohinder Lal scored on a penalty shot. Pakistan won in 1968, defeating Australia. In 1972, West Germany won the field hockey gold medal, besting Pakistan, 1–0, and becoming the first country outside of Asia to win an Olympic field hockey gold medal since England won in 1908. Until then, only India and Pakistan had been Olympic champions.

But India and Pakistan were not ready to give up their domination of the sport. After New Zealand won Olympic gold in 1976, India captured the 1980 gold medal by defeating Spain, 4–3.

Pakistan won the gold again in 1984, defeating Australia, 1–0. A player named Kaleemullah scored the game's only goal in overtime. His goal, the only one he scored during the Olympics, also made history. It was the first time an Olympic field hockey game had been won by an overtime goal. Pakistan's victory was considered an upset because of Australia's long winning streak. Before losing to Pakistan, Australia had not lost a game in two years. Australia had also won five straight international tournaments.

As mentioned earlier, the United States boycotted the Olympic Games in 1980, the year that women's field hockey became an Olympic sport. The women's field hockey team from Zimbabwe took home the gold medal that year.

Stephen Veen (10) of the Netherlands struggles to gain control of the ball as Joaquin Malgosa of Spain tries to steal it away during their gold medal field hockey match at the Centennial Olympic Games held in Atlanta in 1996.

Since 1980, Australia and the Netherlands have become the dominant forces in Olympic women's field hockey. Australia won gold medals in 1988 and 1996. The Netherlands won the gold medal in 1984 and the bronze in 1996. When Australia defeated South Korea, 3–1, for the '96 gold medal, it was the 40th straight win for the team in international competition. Perhaps the Australian women's team will become the next power in Olympic field hockey, the way India's men's team was for most of the 20th century.

In the summer of 1996 the International Hockey Federation changed the system for Olympic qualification. World champion field hockey teams were no longer automatically given a spot at the Olympic Games. The new system was scheduled to take effect for the 2000 Olympics in Sydney, Australia. The International Hockey Federation also adjusted the scoring of field hockey competitions, making a win worth three points instead of two. This change was an attempt to encourage more offensive play in the game.

To promote more scoring, field hockey also dropped its offside rule. Players no longer have to keep the ball or a defender ahead of them while trying to reach a scoring position.

Like the Olympics, the World Cup tournament is an international competition. The first World Cup was won by Pakistan in 1971, when its men's team defeated Spain in overtime. Pakistan and the Netherlands have both dominated men's field hockey World Cup tournaments. Each country has won two gold and two silver medals. Men's teams from the United States have never won a World Cup medal.

Women's World Cup field hockey competition began in 1974, and that year, the Netherlands won the gold medal. Since 1974, the women's team from the Netherlands has dominated World Cup tournaments, winning four gold medals, two silvers, and one bronze. In '74, Holland defeated Argentina, 1–0, when Nel van Kollenburg scored in overtime, after more than 92 minutes of the game had gone by. Van Kollenburg, nicknamed "Big Nel," was playing in the first tournament of her career. In 1994 at Dublin, Ireland, the U.S. women's team won a bronze medal, the first medal ever won by a team from the United States in the World Cup.

Like Canada's exciting 1–0 victory over Argentina in the 1999 Pan Am Games, many of the most exciting field hockey matches have

Hwang Jong-Hyun of South Korea, left, battles for the ball with Ali Raza of Pakistan during the second half in the men's field hockey qualifying tournament in Osaka, Japan, on March 18, 2000. Pakistan beat South Korea, 3–1, but both teams qualified for the Sydney Olympics.

taken place between teams from different nations. During the 1956 Olympics in Melbourne, Australia, Germany and Pakistan were tied, 1–1. Neither team was able to break the tie. With only a few minutes left in the game, a penalty was called against a German player for illegally blocking a shot with his hand. The referee ordered the teams to participate in a bully, or face-off.

This was a tense part of the game, as the winner of the bully could help his team score a goal and win the game. The German player tried to get an advantage against his opponent.

He went after the ball without touching sticks three times. According to the rules of field hockey, players facing off in a bully must tap the ground and one another's sticks three times before the ball can be advanced. The referee caught the German player and ordered another bully to take place. The players lined up a second time. But again, the German player went after the ball too soon. This time, the referee gave Germany a penalty. He awarded Pakistan a goal. No more points were scored in this game. Pakistan won, 2–1, and eventually captured the silver medal.

The 1960 Olympics took place in Rome, Italy. During the field hockey tournament, France and Belgium were engaged in a scoreless match. An Italian police officer on duty outside the field hockey stadium blew his whistle while directing traffic. The noise was so loud that the Belgian players thought the umpire had blown his whistle instead, which would have been a signal to stop playing. They stopped and looked for the umpire to tell them why play was halted. But the French team did not stop. Seeing their opponents suddenly standing still, the French players roared through the Belgians and scored a goal. That turned out to be the only score of the game, which the French won, 1–0. The Belgian players learned a valuable lesson: don't be distracted by noises during games. Until the umpire or referee tells you to stop, keep on playing.

After losing the gold medal to West Germany in the 1972 Olympics, the Pakistani players were very angry and upset. During the ceremony when medals were awarded, several

Pakistani players refused to face the German flag during the playing of that country's national anthem. This was very poor behavior in the Olympics, where good sportsmanship is expected. As a punishment for their behavior, the Pakistani players were banned from future Olympic Games. Eventually, they were allowed to return to the Olympics, competing in 1976 and winning the bronze medal.

At the Centennial Olympic Games held in Atlanta, Georgia, in 1996, the Netherlands' men's field hockey team took home the gold, followed by the men's teams from Spain and Australia, who won the silver and bronze medals, respectively.

At the beginning of the 21st century, field hockey boasted a number of important tournaments and events, including the World Cup, the European Nations Cup, the Champions Trophy, the Sultan Azlan Shah Tournament, the Americas Cup, the Africa Cup, the Asia Cup, the Pan American Games, and, of course, the Olympic Games.

Twelve men's teams were slated to compete at the 2000 Olympics in Sydney, Australia, including Australia, which was automatically eligible as the host nation, the Netherlands, which was eligible as the defending nation, and Canada, Great Britain, Spain, South Korea, Pakistan, Malaysia, South Africa, India, Poland, and Germany. The 10 women's field hockey competitors at the 2000 Olympics included Australia, South Korea, Argentina, Germany, New Zealand, the Netherlands, China, Great Britain, Spain, and South Africa.

Field hockey, one of the oldest sports still being played, has provided its fans with many great games to enjoy over the years. As we have seen, defense, solid goalkeeping, and quick scores make field hockey matches exciting to watch and interesting to play. With more than 100 nations playing this sport and many of the best players coming from countries as differ-ent as India, the Netherlands, Spain, and Australia, field hockey is truly an international game.

CHRONOLOGY

2000 B.C.	The earliest record of a field hockey game is painted in Egypt for the tomb of Beni-Hasen.
776 B.C.	The first Olympic Games are held in Greece.
1849 A.D.	The first men's field hockey club, named Blackheath, is formed in England.
1886	The first field hockey league, the Hockey Association, is formed in England.
1887	The first women's field hockey team is started in the town of East Mosley, England.
1889	The first women's field hockey league, the All England Women's Hockey Association, is established.
1901	Constance Applebee introduces American women to field hockey.
1908	Men's field hockey is played in the modern Olympic games for the first time; England wins the gold medal.
1928–1960	India dominates the Olympics in field hockey.
1980	Women's field hockey games are played in the Olympics for the first time; Zimbabwe wins the first gold medal.
1981	Constance Applebee, the mother of field hockey in the United States, dies at the age of 107.
1984	The U.S. women's field hockey team wins a bronze medal in the Olympics.
1994	The U.S. women's team wins a bronze medal at the Women's World Cup competition.
1999	Canada beats Argentina for the Pan American gold medal, marking one of the most exciting games in the history of the sport.
2000	Twelve men's teams and 10 women's teams comprise field hockey competition at the 2000 Olympics at Sydney, Australia.

GLOSSARY

Attacker
A player on the team that possesses the ball.

Bully
Like an ice hockey face-off, it involves two players at the center of the field. They face each other, standing over the ball. They must hit the ground and each other's sticks alternately three times before hitting the ball. A bully is used when the game is stopped for certain reasons by the referee.

Centerline
This is the halfway point on the 100-yard-long field hockey playing field.

Defender
A player on the team without the ball, trying to keep the other team from scoring a goal.

Goal cage
There are two, one at each end of the field. Players shoot balls into the cages to score goals. Each cage has one goalkeeper.

Goalkeeper
Each team has one goalkeeper, whose job is to stop opponents from scoring. This is the only player on the field who can touch the ball with any part of the body, but this can only be done inside the striking circle. If the goalkeeper touches the ball with anything other than the stick outside the circle, this is a foul.

Penalty corner or short corner
A foul awarded by the referee; a player gets a free shot standing at least 10 yards from the goal. Five defenders start from behind the goal line to prevent the attacking team from scoring.

Penalty stroke

A foul awarded by the referee; a player gets a free shot standing seven yards from the goal. The attacker can only touch the ball once, when the shot is taken.

Striking circle

There are two on the field, one in front of each goal. Each circle extends 16 yards into the field. Players must shoot the ball within the circle for a goal to count.

STATISTICS

India's record of Olympic victories and gold medals is one of the greatest achievements in the modern history of team sports. It is unusual for one country to dominate a sport for as long as India did. Here is a chart showing the score of each game and the opponents India defeated in Olympic field hockey competition from 1928–1960.

1928	1932	1936	1948	1952	1956	1960
India—6 Australia—0	India—11 Japan—1	India—4 Hungary—0	India—8 Australia—0	India—4 Australia—0	India—14 Afghanistan—0	India—10 Denmark—0
India—9 Belgium—0	India—24 U.S.A.—1	India—7 U.S.A.—0	India—9 Argentina—1	India—3 England—1	India—16 U.S.A.—0	India—4 Holland—1
India—5 Denmark—0		India—9 Japan—0	India—2 Spain—0	India—6 Holland—1	India—6 Singapore—0	India—3 New Zealand—0
India—5 Switzerland—0		India—10 France—0	India—2 Holland—1		India—1 W. Germany—0	India—1 Australia—0
India—3 Holland—0		India—8 Germany—1	India—4 England—0		India—1 Pakistan—0	India—1 W. Germany—0

FURTHER READING

Anders, Beth, with Sue Myers. *Field Hockey—Steps to Success*. Champaign, Illinois: Human Kinetics Publishing, 1999.

Hickok, Ralph. *A Who's Who of Sports Champions*. New York: Houghton Mifflin & Co., 1995.

Laing, Jane, editor. *Chronicle of the Olympics, 1896-1996*. New York: DK Publishing, 1996.

Markel, Robert, Marcella Smith, and Susan Waggoner, editors. *The Women's Sports Encyclopedia*. New York: Henry Holt & Co. Inc., 1997.

Wallechinsky, David. *The Complete Book of the Olympics*. New York: The Penguin Group, 1988.

INTERNET RESOURCES
www.usfieldhockey.com - USA Field Hockey

SPECIAL COLLECTIONS
Adele H. Boyd Collections at Ursinus College, Collegeville, Pennsylvania

INDEX

BRUCE ADELSON has written several books for children, including *The Composite Guide to Softball* (Chelsea House Publishers, 2000), and *Grand Slam Trivia, Slam Dunk Trivia, Hat Trick Trivia,* and *Touchdown Trivia* (Lerner Books, 1998). His books for adults include *The Minor League Baseball Book* (Macmillan, 1995) and *Brushing Back Jim Crow: The Integration of Minor League Baseball in the American South* (University Press of Virginia, 1999). Bruce has also been a commentator for National Public Radio's *Morning Edition* and CBS Radio's *Major League Baseball Game of the Week* and the contributing editor for *The Four Sports Stadium Guide* (Random House, 1994). Bruce has also written about sports and other topics for *The Washington Post, Atlanta Journal-Constitution, Baseball America, Sport Magazine, USA Today's Baseball Weekly, The Daily Record, Baseball Digest,* and *Maryland Magazine.*

A book and multimedia reviewer for *Children's Literature,* Bruce is also a former practicing trial lawyer with 10 years of litigation experience and a former elementary school substitute teacher in Arlington, Virginia.